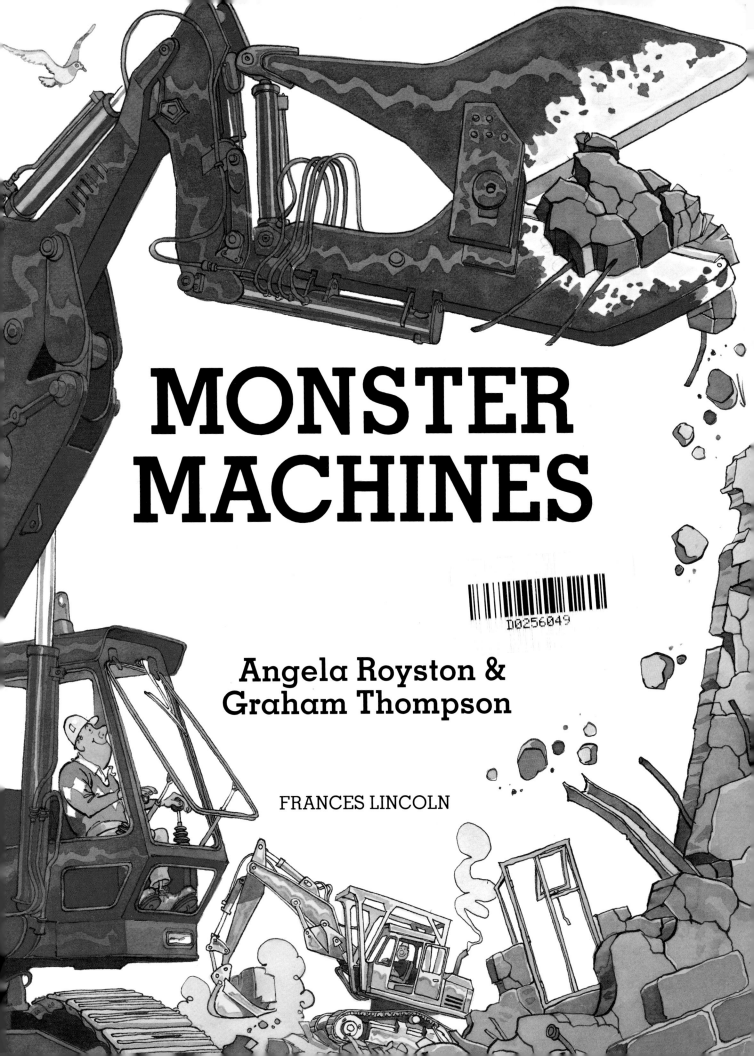

MONSTER MACHINES

Angela Royston &
Graham Thompson

FRANCES LINCOLN

Crusher

These old houses are being knocked down to make way for a new building.
The giant crusher grips a whole floor between its huge jaws and **crash** – bricks, plaster and concrete come tumbling down!

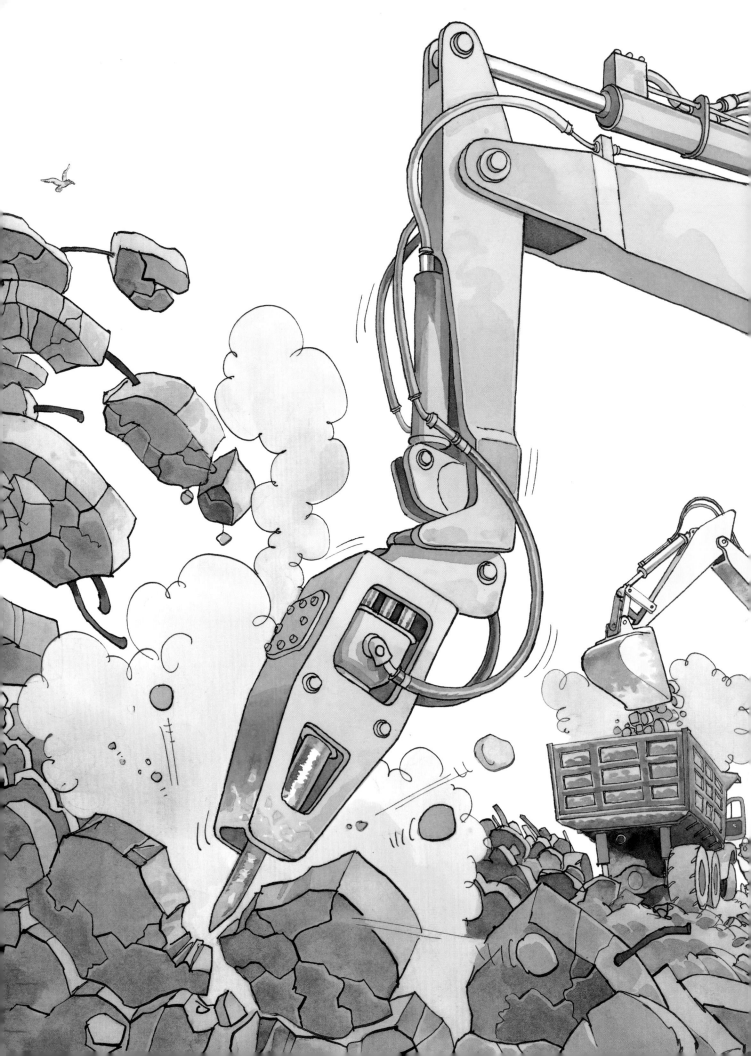

Breaker

This powerful breaker smashes the big lumps of concrete into smaller pieces. Then the rubble is scooped into trucks and taken away. At last the site is cleared and ready for building to begin.

Piling rig

The piling rigs drill deep into the ground. They are making big holes for the foundations of the new building. This giant corkscrew is lifting out a column of mud. Watch out – as it spins around, the mud flies off!

Concrete mixer

Along comes the concrete mixer. Its huge
drum turns slowly round and round
to keep the concrete runny.
A heavy metal beam has been dropped
into the hole made by the piling rig.
Now concrete is pouring in to fill up the
hole. When it has set hard it will make a
really strong foundation for the building.

Tower crane

The tower crane builds the skyscraper's steel frame higher and higher.
The driver lowers the hook and picks up a beam.
Then he swings it round to the men who are waiting to bolt it into place.

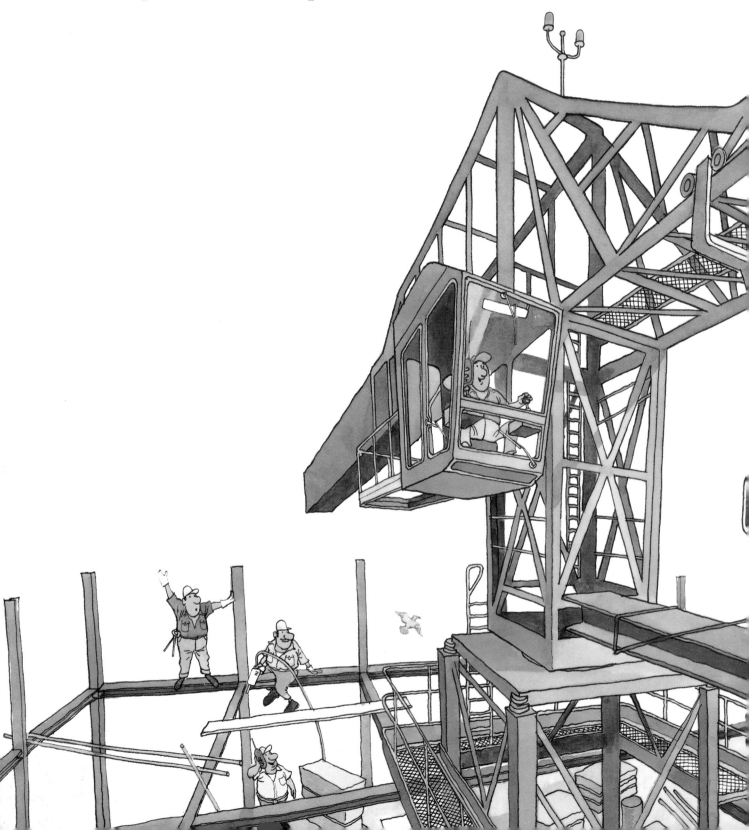

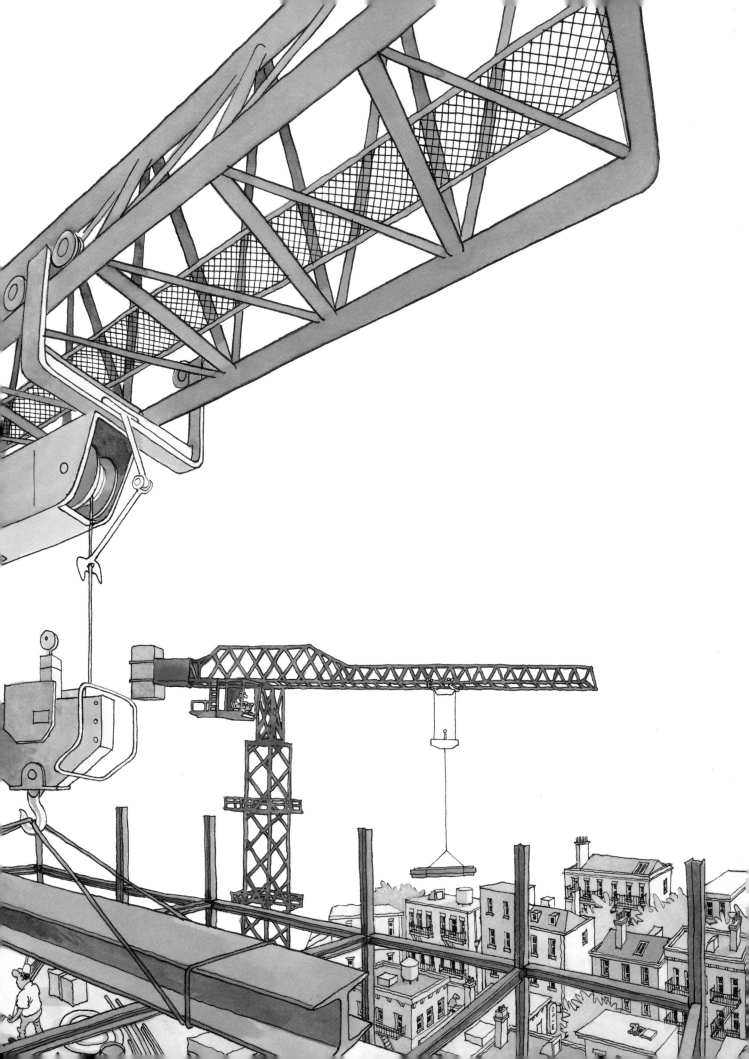

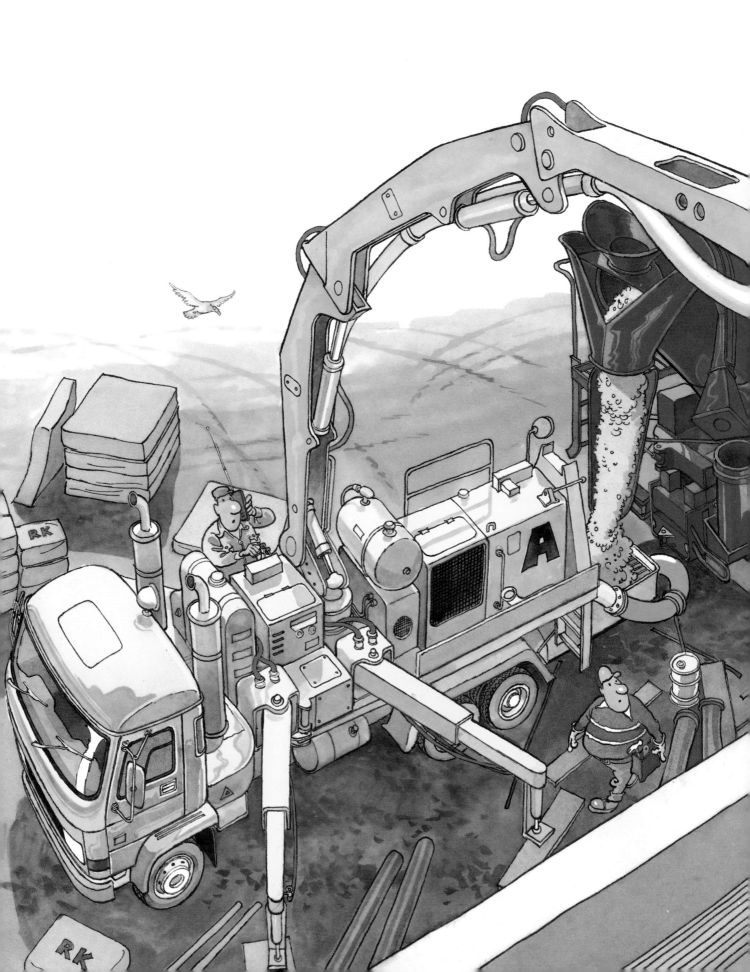

Concrete pump

Now the men are ready to make the concrete floors. The mixer cannot reach by itself so it feeds the concrete pump instead. The pump's long pipe reaches right up into the building.

Hoist

These men are putting up a hoist. It will lift things up and down the outside of the building.

The men slot in the pieces, then move the cab up, ready to put in the next piece. Soon they are so high above the ground the trucks and houses below look very small.

Lorry loader

This truck is delivering walls and windows. The truck's crane lifts the window and lowers it carefully on to a stack, ready for the tower crane to swing it into place.

Mobile crane

The big machines have finished their
work. Now the mobile crane moves in
to take down the tower crane piece
by piece.

The new skyscraper is finished at last!

Bulldozer

Outside the town, more monster machines
have come to build a new road.
This powerful bulldozer is clearing
a way through rocks and earth. Its
caterpillar tracks grip the rough
ground and the bulldozer slowly
pushes forward. Trees and bushes
come crashing down.

Scraper

The scraper is clearing the ground. Its big blade slices the earth and pushes it into the bowl.
Here comes the bulldozer to help move the scraper along.

Excavator

These excavators are loading earth into dumper trucks.
The bucket reaches out and scoops up some earth. Then the huge arm lifts and swings the bucket over to the dumper truck. The bucket tips and the earth drops into the truck.

Dumper truck

The dumper truck takes the earth to fill in a
dip in the road.
The back of the truck tilts up and
the earth tumbles out.

Motor-grader

This machine makes the road smooth.
Its heavy blade scrapes away bumps
and fills in holes.
The blade is tilted so that the road will
slope down at the sides and rain will run
off it.

Digger

This digger is making a ditch beside the road for rainwater to drain into. The bucket and boom dig up the earth like a vast metal hand and arm.

Paver

Now the road is ready to be tarred.
The hot sticky asphalt slides slowly out of
the tipper lorry into the paver. The paver
spreads it over the road.

Road-roller

The road-roller follows close behind the paver. Its shuddering black drum presses down the hot asphalt.
The asphalt cools to make a tough hard surface for cars and trucks to drive on.

Road-marker

This machine sprays white lines onto the road. The lines show drivers where they can go.
Now the road is finished at last.

Can you spot these monster machines for yourself?
Have a look next time you go out!

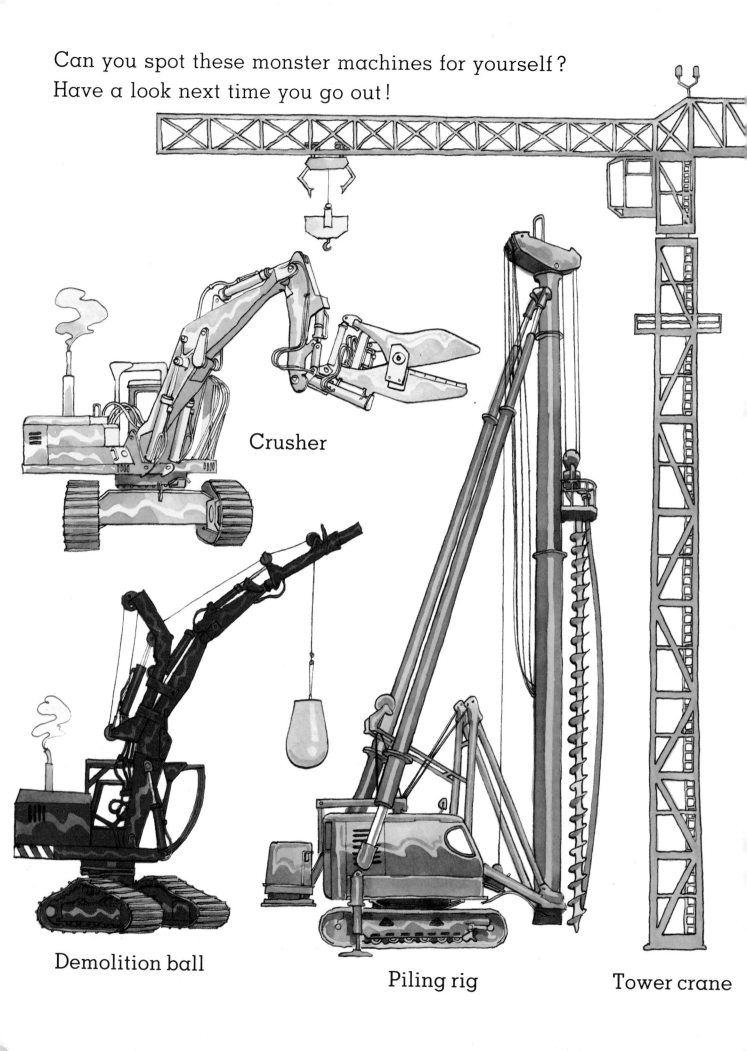

Crusher

Demolition ball

Piling rig

Tower crane

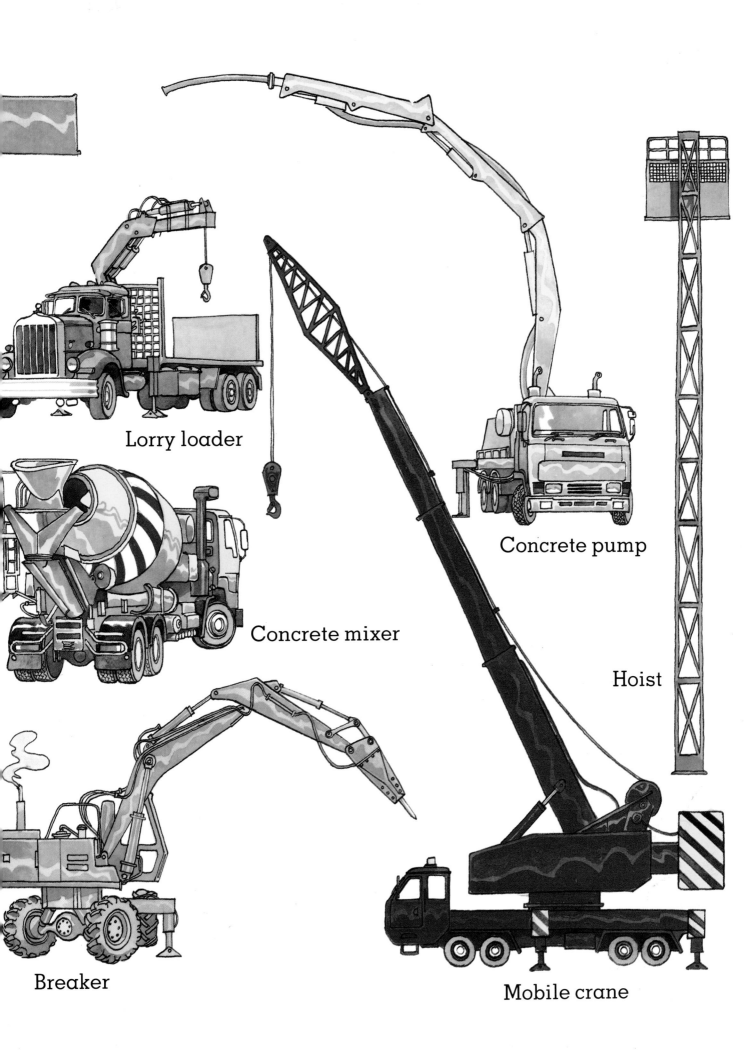

Lorry loader

Concrete mixer

Breaker

Concrete pump

Hoist

Mobile crane

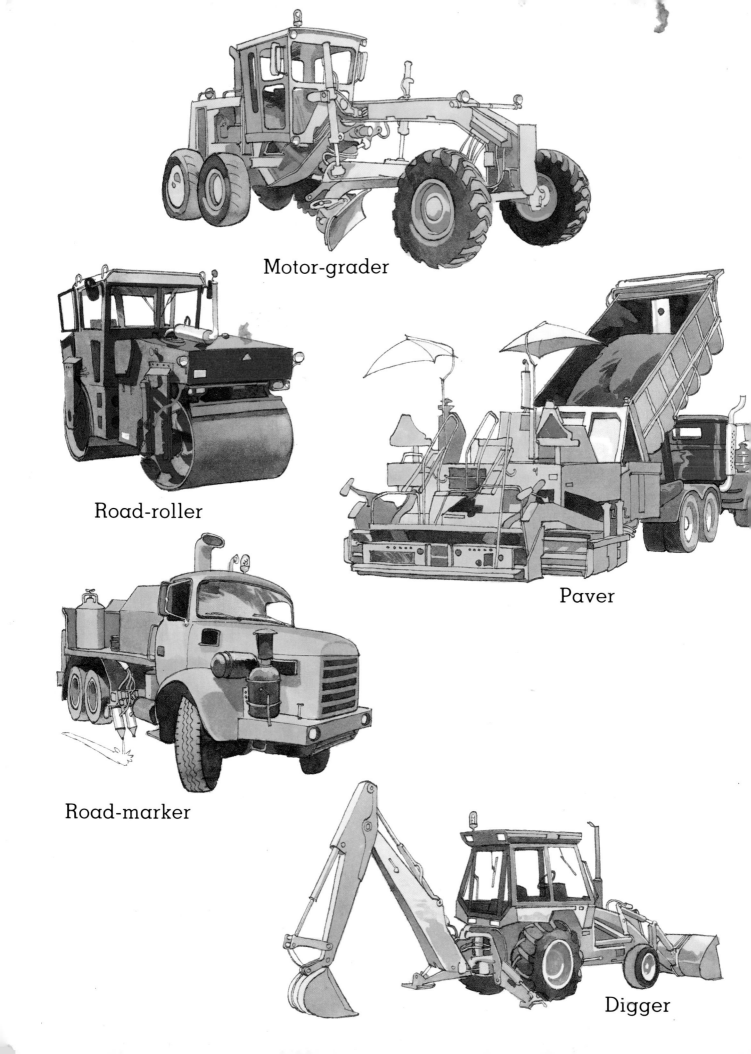

Motor-grader

Road-roller

Paver

Road-marker

Digger